Take Back Your Life!

Rosemarie Rossetti, Ph.D.

FORTUNA PRESS

Fortuna Press | Columbus, Ohio

Take Back Your Life!

Rosemarie@RosemarieSpeaks.com
http://www.RosemarieSpeaks.com

ISBN 0-9741550-0-4
Library of Congress Control Number: 2003094240

Published by Fortuna Press
http://www.FortunaPress.com
Editor@FortunaPress.com

First Edition

Take Back Your Life!
Regaining Your Footing After Life Throws You a Curve

Rosemarie Rossetti, Ph.D.

Acknowledgments

I thank the members of the "Dream Team" who are responsible for the production of this book. Each of them was passionate about this project and contributed in their own special way. Located in different parts of the country, this group communicated well together, shared ideas and their talents in order to bring this book to the marketplace.

Wendy Hardman took the lead, assembled the team of designers, and helped in the selection of the articles. Jason Dickens is the artistic mind responsible for the cover design. Julie Driscoll selected all of the artistic components to arrange my words and graphics on the pages. Claire Gerus, editor, took my original articles and crafted them into a polished manuscript. As a writing coach, she taught me how to more clearly compose my thoughts and share my emotions.

To my husband, Mark Leder, I thank you for your perpetual love and support. You have encouraged me and served as my sounding board when ideas for articles came to my mind. I appreciate the time you took listening while I read aloud the original draft of each article, and for your constructive feedback.

Table of Contents

Introduction

On June 13, 1998, I lay on a bicycle path, paralyzed in fear, after being crushed by a 3 ½ ton tree. Little did I know that my experiences after recovering from a spinal cord injury would bring me life-changing insights. While still in my hospital bed, I was encouraged to write and record my thoughts. At the time it gave me a focus – something to do. Later it would serve as a personal journal of my recovery.

Now, I offer these reflections to you to read, absorb, re-read, and reflect upon. While in the hospital, I was surrounded by friends and family who had come to support, encourage, and love me. Many sent me flowers as a symbol of their love and concern for my recovery. My hospital room looked like and smelled like a florist's shop, and I loved each and every flower, however I was especially drawn to the roses.

Roses always bring back childhood memories of my parents, Fiorovante and Rose Rossetti. Both of them loved roses and grew them in their garden. Every evening, my father would come home from work and cut a rose off the climbing rose bush at the back door. Before entering the kitchen, he would remove the thorns and jauntily place the rose behind his ear. I remember seeing him smiling as he came in to greet us.

My love for gardening was also nurtured by my mother as she encouraged me to help her care for her roses. When I went to high school, I took a class in horticulture and loved it! In college, I majored in horticulture and agricultural education. I decided I wanted to teach others how to work with and enjoy plants.

When I became a professional speaker and trainer in 1997, I selected the rose for my logo. Now, every time I see a rose, I am drawn to it, taking in its beauty and fragrance.

What special image or symbol has meaning for you? What inspires, calms or helps you heal when your energy is low? By bringing that image into your mind you, too, may experience a sense of hope and renewal. And, if no other image comes to mind, I offer you my rose. May it help you move forward, day by day, until you, too, have taken back your life.

1

Touched by Fate:
How My Life Changed in an Instant

It was Saturday, June 13, 1998, a glorious day for many reasons. My husband, Mark and I were celebrating our third wedding anniversary, and the weather was beautiful – warm and windless.

We decided to go for a bicycle ride on a trail in Granville, Ohio, and arrived about 5:00 p.m. We were happily riding along for about ten minutes when Mark heard a loud noise that sounded like a gunshot. He slowed down to investigate, then called ahead to me, "Look over there, something's falling!" I glanced to my right and saw a few leaves floating to the ground. Then Mark yelled, "Stop!"

It was too late. An 80-foot tree was falling on our path. In an instant, I was crushed by a 3 ½ ton tree and surrounded by live electric power lines.

Neither of us knew that our lives would be forever changed by this freak occurrence. All I could do was try to cope with unbearable pain. Mark was frantic, but managed to contain his fear so as not to further frighten me. When the paramedics arrived, I was flown by helicopter to the hospital where surgeons rushed me to the operating room.

They discovered that the tree had crushed five vertebra in my back, two in my neck, and injured my spinal cord. Doctors implanted metal rods in my back and grafted bone from my hip to my back to stabilize my spine.

I spent five mind-numbing days in Intensive Care and five more weeks in a rehabilitation center. While working with my physical therapists, I told them, "I want my life back!" I asked them to work with me and teach me how to regain strength and function. My progress was very slow. I realized that any gains I could make would result from my taking charge of my own life. My persistence and dogged determination were exactly what the doctor ordered, and helped me in my recovery.

When I came home, my life was transformed. I was not able to work due to my injury and I spent the next two years in physical and occupational therapy, three days a week. I also worked every day at home on stretching and strengthening exercises. After about a year, I began a cardio and weight-training program at the health club.

> *"In an instant, I was crushed by a 3 ½ ton tree and surrounded by live electric power lines."*

In December 1999, I began writing the inspirational articles that appear in this book. Every month, I would share on my website and in print media, the life lessons I was learning, as well as insights on coping with change and recovering from adversity. These articles allow me to share my personal story with you, and to provide you with a fresh perspective about life. They also demonstrate how you, too, can live your life with conviction.

2

Adversity Brings Personal Growth

We all experience crises in our lives. Setbacks such as illness, divorce, layoffs, and deaths in our families often come unexpectedly. Our future happiness and success are determined by how we react to our misfortunes. By observing others, we can learn how to become more resilient when adversity strikes.

As a survivor of a life-changing event, I have learned from experience how to bounce back in the face of adversity. Lost is my ability to stand or walk without the aid of crutches, something most of us take for granted. I am dependent on my wheelchair for getting around the house and my community. Coping with the losses of this tragedy has been the greatest challenge I have ever faced.

What do you do when your world comes crashing down, when all your hopes and dreams are shattered? Suddenly, your life is rocked to the core, and you must look within to find strength. A large dose of self-determination and tenacity can project you forward.

In order to restore my independence, which I so desperately wanted to regain, I had to learn to do many things all over again. Simple tasks like dressing and showering seemed impossible. My guiding motivation was that a better future lay ahead. I vowed to do whatever was necessary to move towards restoring function and mobility in my body.

In the past year and a half, I have gained new insights into how to step forward after adversity changed my life. I discovered that by setting goals, I could make more progress. Written goals will help you progress toward your objective. Make a mental note of what small steps you need to initiate and accomplish in order to achieve your goals.

In my continuing journey of recovery and rehabilitation, I have learned many lessons that I have turned into rules to live by. One simple guideline I follow in order to accomplish my goals is to do something new every day. No matter how small the activity, each one counts. You are the judge. Each new pursuit should be in line with your goals.

An example of a new task I was determined to master was putting on my shoes while lying in bed. I had relearned how to dress myself, but was still unable to put on my own shoes. Because my feet are paralyzed, I had to use my hands to position my shoes on my feet. First, I had to grab one leg and pull it across the other at the knee. Then I had to pick up my shoe and position it on my foot. I repeated the same process with the other leg until both shoes were on. However, I could only achieve this after strengthening and flexing the muscles in my legs so I could actually bring my foot over to my knee. This required my performing a series of exercises every day at home until I had developed the necessary strength and flexibility. Each day brought me closer to the joy of victory. After about a month of practicing, I was finally able to completely dress myself.

The act of doing something new every day needs to be a conscious habit. Upon awakening in the morning, before getting out of bed, focus on what the new activity will be for that day. If nothing comes to mind, allow your subconscious mind to work on it throughout the day. It is important that you keep returning to the thought of doing something new, then take action to complete the task.

This may be hard to accomplish at first. The day can get away from you. Do what you can in the time remaining before you sleep. The next morning, start contemplating an activity you can reasonably accomplish that day.

You may find yourself resisting new activities. Sometimes we put up mental roadblocks and say, "I can't." Recognize when you mentally limit your pursuits because you believe that you can't accomplish the task. What at first seems impossible, may turn out to be very possible!

It is important to recognize your progress and take pride in your accomplishments. Share your achievements with others. Brag a little, and allow the recognition and support of those around you to nurture you.

Adversity precedes growth. As you start working towards your goals and realizing progress, you will be encouraged to attempt even more challenging activities in the days ahead.

Take time to look back. Looking back teaches you how far you have come, and reinforces your belief in your abilities. Soon you will see that the crisis in your life has brought you new insights and meaning. You will become different after having faced the adversity. You may even find that the changes you make as a result of your life crisis will bring you closer to fulfilling your goals and realizing your dreams.

3

Love and the Meaning of Life

"*What man actually needs is not a tensionless state but rather the striving and struggling for some goal worthy of him.*"
— *Viktor Frankl*

Has your world ever come crashing down on you? Mine did, literally and figuratively when a 3 1/2 ton tree fell and crushed me while I was riding my bicycle. I became paralyzed from the waist down. We all can look back at our lives and remember times of horror, panic, and grief.

A major turning point in my recovery occurred while reading, "Man's Search for Meaning." This is a story written by psychiatrist Viktor Frankl, a German concentration camp survivor.

I read this book a few months after coming home from the hospital. I was depressed and having a

> *"Although I had considered ending my life, I now realized that I wanted to survive – and in time, thrive – for those I loved."*

difficult time coping with life changes. All of my life goals had to be readjusted. At times I found little meaning for life. I was in pain a great deal of the time and my ability to function was severely limited.

My spirit needed a boost. Then came the epiphany. As I read Frankl's story, I understood one of his central themes: "For what matters above all is the attitude we take toward suffering, the attitude in which we take our suffering upon ourselves." I found that these words reawakened my sense of purpose for living. Before now I hadn't really suffered. This unbearable pain was bringing new meaning to me. Although I had considered ending my life, I now realized that I wanted to survive, and in time, thrive, for those I loved. Although all else had been stripped away – my function, my independence, and my life style – I could still control my attitude. I could be negative or positive, withdrawn or loving.

Viktor Frankl believed love is the ultimate goal to which man can aspire, in fact it was his salvation. When in a position of utter desperation, being in love and being loved became the fuel to inspire him back into life.

The love for my husband, mother, brothers, family, and friends gave me the power to push my life forward. The thoughts of them loving me and me loving them provided comfort and inspiration for living.

> *"The love for my husband, mother, brothers, family, and friends gave me the power to push my life forward."*

As you reflect upon what your absence would mean to those who love you, you will realize that your existence has value. Your goal in life can be redefined by the loving role you play in the lives of others.

As you bounce back from a tragedy, you will need the loving support of others. This is a time for you to receive all the love that is available. Listen to the loving words of encouragement from others. Have a persistent determination to rebound and come back stronger. Come back to love.

What may at first seem to be an insurmountable challenge can be achieved. Approach each day with an "I Can Do It!" attitude. Let your love for others fuel your passion to get on with your life.

4

Getting Back to 'Normal'

For all of us, life is unpredictable and uncertain. Illness, injury, loss of a loved one, work changes, divorce, and bankruptcy can lead to a sudden realization that our lives have changed. After the life-changing event, we are resistant, wanting our lives back again the way they were. We want to be "normal" again. We want our lives to be as they were: fully functioning, doing the things we used to do, sleeping through the night, eating. We shudder at the thought that we will never be "normal" again.

My life drastically changed after I became paralyzed from the waist down, and I grieved my loss and desperately clung to thoughts of returning to the life I had lived before my injury. I told my physical therapist, "I want my life back," and struggled each day as I tried to do my daily self care and become more mobile.

What I have learned is that "normal" can be defined by each individual and redefined throughout life. As we change, so should our perceptions of what is "normal." Now as a person with a disability, I am no longer able to do certain things like walk, jog, and swim. However, being disabled doesn't mean that I am not "normal." I got my life back, but the chances of getting it back exactly as it was before my injury are highly unlikely.

Life for me has returned to "normal." In fact, I have a new standard of "normal." Now, I drive a van with hand controls and get around in my wheelchair. I've had to give up doing some things and substitute these with others. I have returned to my career as a speaker and writer, and I am making a living. I have a loving relationship with my husband. I take care of our home, travel, and enjoy recreational sports. I have my life back. It's just different now.

As you look at your life after adversity, think about what returning to "normal" would mean for you. What modifications in your lifestyle will need to be made? What adaptations would help you to be more productive? What would make you happy again? What is limiting you from getting your life back? What can you do to take the first step towards getting back to "normal"?

It may be time to redefine what is "normal." Living your life differently doesn't mean you are abnormal. You must be willing to accept how things are for now, and move on. Your attitude about making these changes must be positive, and you must be open to all possibilities.

> *"I have my life back. It's just different now."*

You are probably not the only person who has experienced your particular situation. There are others who have learned how to make the necessary changes and get on with their lives. They learned how to redefine "normal." You can use others as role models so you too can take back your life.

"Normal" people are well adjusted, capable of adapting to life and what comes their way – even if it means making the best of a challenging situation.

5

Balancing Your Wheel of Life

In nature, where there is balance, there is harmony. Nature continually seeks balance. Human nature too strives for balance. When life is out of balance, we can become unhappy.

Life is too short to spend it being unhappy. It can end or change in an instant. It should be enjoyed, savored, and cherished with each day. For some people, life is richly rewarding. For others, life just moves along with missing pieces and deep voids. Sometimes these voids go undetected for years, robbing us of life's pleasures.

Several months after my spinal cord injury, I attended a seminar where the wheel of life graphic was explained. Life is very much like this wheel. A wheel rolls when it is in balance. A lopsided wheel is unable to go forward. When life gets out of balance, adjustments are necessary in order to stabilize it.

To assess how much in balance your life is, look at which segments of the wheel of life are deficient. This can help explain why you may have been feeling the blues. If you have been feeling as if something is missing in your life, it may be found in one or more of the eight segments.

Get out your colored pens and fill in each of the segments of the wheel of life. Those that are abundant need to be filled in more completely. Those segments that are totally deficient, leave blank. If a segment is somewhat lacking in your life, partially color in the segment.

When I colored in my wheel of life, I was stunned to realize that there was no fun in my life! All the fun things I did before my injury, I could no longer do, and I was depressed due to my loss. My life lacked vitality. All the sporting and recreational activities that I once enjoyed had kept my life in balance. Now that these activities were missing from my life, I had to find a way to replace them by learning how to have fun again.

wheel of Life

Physical Environment, Career, Fun & Recreation, Money, Personal Growth, Health, Sig. Other/Romance, Friends & Family

This realization was a major turning point in my recovery. I began actively exploring adaptive sports and recreation programs that were appropriate for my abilities. I wanted to restore my life balance, and I knew that happiness would return when I did. That meant that I had to learn a new way to play tennis, racquetball and golf; go biking, snow skiing, ice skating, kayaking, snorkeling, horseback riding, and snowmobiling.

I also made a decision to go to sporting events, movies, picnics, parties, special events, concerts, and the theatre. My husband and I began going out on dates with each other again and eating out in restaurants. The activities that I could no longer do, like rollerblading, needed a substitute activity. I was open to possibilities and tried new activities every chance I got.

Sometimes people get so caught up in raising their family and building their careers, they neglect to have fun in their lives. To keep their lifes in balance, people should schedule fun activities like hobbies, sports, or going to the health club.

As we recognize what segments of our wheel of life need our attention, we need to write goals and begin to work towards them. For me, it meant making a few phone calls and scheduling time to try out new adaptive equipment and receive instruction.

Examine your life balance. Work towards the one segment that is most deficient, that will make the most impact. As you focus on one of the eight components, it is also important to be grateful for the other components of your life, and not take them for granted.

Research what you will need to do to get started. Make a plan. Have some clear goals in mind that you can measure as time goes on, so you can see your progress. Be aware of how good it feels as you accomplish these goals. Each success can fuel future successes.

It's time to restore balance to your wheel of life. When you do, you'll enjoy the get-up-and-go, energy, and enthusiasm for life that you had before. Best of all, you'll appreciate them more than ever!

6

Fear Can Be the Fuel for Courage

I went skiing this past weekend. For most people, this is not a big deal. For me, this is a big deal, since I am paralyzed.

Skiers who cannot use their legs ski in a "monoski." It is like riding in a sled on one ski. There is a place to sit and a place to put your feet. Your legs are stretched out in front of you. Two outrigger poles are used to steer and to brake. They resemble forearm crutches. At the end of the pole is a foot long ski tip that moves up and down.

During this first lesson, I was scared – scared of falling, scared of getting hurt. I had felt that same fear twenty-four years ago when I first learned how to ski, then skiing on both legs. Now, the mountain seemed so steep! Gravity was not my friend. Skiing was so different. Learning was hard. During the lesson, my shoulders, wrists, arms and neck ached. "What fun is this?" I asked myself as I struggled to steer the contraption.

> *"Courage is doing what you're afraid to do. There can be no courage unless you're scared."*
>
> —Eddie Rickenbacker

Then I remembered the joy from my past. Memories of all those ski holidays with friends and family came into view as I looked up at the ski slope. My motivation to learn anew was the deep-seated belief that I could ski again. I needed to find courage to face my fears.

The famed World War II pilot, Eddie Rickenbacker, once said,

13

"Courage is doing what you're afraid to do. There can be no courage unless you're scared."

It is time to face the obstacles we have been avoiding. Sometimes we are not even aware that we have been steering clear of barriers until we open our eyes and examine the way we live, day by day. With renewed awareness, mindful of our hesitations, we will recognize what we have to do to change.

From time to time, you will face fearful situations. Often you will avoid going forward, and revert to your old ways. Many times you will dismiss the thought that you can overcome your fears.

I have learned that there are many obstacles to face in life. Often, I think I can't do things because of my disability.

Over the years I've learned that it is better to be courageous and confront my obstacles. I look at the risks involved and the steps that would be necessary to accomplish the task. Then I break the task down into manageable pieces. I eliminate as many of the risks as I can before I begin, and I start working on positive self-talk.

Phrases that work for me are: "I can do this. It is not that hard. I'm making progress. This is fun. I will do this." By focusing on these words, I become motivated and confident that I will reach my objective.

See yourself succeeding as you approach difficult tasks. Picture yourself at the "bottom of the hill," that special time and place when you have successfully completed the task.

Acknowledge your apprehension, and think about achieving your goal. Do not let any self doubt enter your mind. Block it out. Always believe in yourself. Always expect the best.

As we feel fear deep within, we should use it to move us forward. Courageous acts are fueled by fear. Fear can paralyze or fear can mobilize. It's really up to us!

7

Bouncing Back

How do you handle uncertainty? What is your reaction when you hear bad news about your health or your loved one's health, the stock market, the economy, the nation's health and security?

We are living in very uncertain times. We feel great apprehension as we read newspapers and watch news broadcasts. Oftentimes we are stunned, and panicked. When things hit us unexpectedly, there is no time to catch our breath.

We fear for our future and cringe at how our world has changed. We look for answers, comfort, security, hope, stability, and peace. We want to fully recover, fast.

Sometimes our world comes crashing down on us. I have learned many lessons from this tragic event as I struggle to get my life back. As I reflect on what helped me to rebound from my crisis, I learned much about the resilient spirit.

> *"The ability to rebound faster is connected to our resiliency..."*

Within each of us is the ability to rebound from bad news, tragedy, and setbacks. As we process the reality of what has happened, we initially assess our losses and examine how our lives will be changed. We see our world crumbling down around us.

The ability to rebound faster is connected to our resiliency – our ability to be flexible, to adapt to change, to see hope in our future. Change is constant and we must be open to possibilities. Not all change is bad. We have to see past the tragedy, crisis, or setback and realize that life at this time may look bleak, but there will be better tomorrows.

Our ability to envision a brighter future will help keep our spirits high.

Too often, people are dehydrated in spirit – overwhelmed by the complications in their lives, and unable to think clearly. They are affected by their environment and the company they keep. They feel emotionally drained and unable to solve their problems.

Resilient people go into a problem-solving mode quickly. They investigate the facts of the situation and gather as much information as possible. They look back at history and study the trends. Often, they consult with others to better identify and understand the problem. They seek the wisdom of others who have been through similar situations. Once they understand the situation, they feel more empowered. Armed with information, they can make decisions and take action.

Resilient people have a supportive network of friends, family, and colleagues who lend a hand and offer encouragement along the way. This group of allies helps to boost their spirits.

To evaluate your own resiliency, take note of your willingness to do new things. Also look at your ability to modify or change how you do things. Examine your history of depression after a setback. See how long it takes you to seek out information, or to take action to resolve your problems or challenges. You cannot guarantee certainty in your life, but you can make your spirit more resilient as your react to uncertain times.

8

Pain Can Be a Gift

Sometimes life brings you a bowl of lemons for you to make lemonade. As we live our roller coaster-like experiences, we are faced with challenges, pain, hardships, and frustrations followed by happiness, elation, and growth.

When we look at our more painful experiences, we often realize that these are lessons life has taught us. For many of us, school is always in session. We are continuously aware that through all of our hardships we come out of the experience a little stronger and wiser. We see the experience as an opportunity to learn life lessons.

I must remind myself each time I am disappointed, frustrated, and upset. I must come away from the experience and ask myself, "What did this teach me?"

Sometimes experiences are costly. Time is wasted, money is lost, and feelings are hurt. The value of the lesson learned need not be in direct proportion to our loses, however. We must be in a state of mind to reflect upon what this experience has shown us so that we will live a more successful and happy future.

We can all learn from our mistakes. We live and learn. This past weekend I went on a horseback ride. This had been a part of my physical therapy program a year ago. This time was different. I went to a public stable and joined a group of 15 other riders to enjoy a Sunday afternoon in the country.

When I met the tour guide and signed up for the ride, I told him that I was paralyzed from the waist down, but could ride a gentle horse if it walked slowly. He brought out a horse named Red.

My husband, Mark, and the tour guide assisted me out of my

wheelchair as I put my arms around Mark's neck and was lifted onto the saddle. The tour guide positioned my legs and put my feet in the stirrups.

As I sat tall in the saddle, I smiled with the anticipation of being on a horse that walked. Since I couldn't walk, I was able to get around on this horse's back, the next best thing to walking.

The group prepared to leave the stable area on its tour. I heard the tour guide asking Mark if I could ride a slow trot. Mark told him he thought I could, since I had some riding experience. The horses followed the lead tour guide in single file. My horse walked near the end of the line.

It was a cool, cloudy day, so I wore my jacket, tennis shoes and jeans. I also wore a helmet, just in case I should fall. I looked back and smiled at Mark, who rode behind me on his horse. This was our day to enjoy.

After about five minutes of riding, I noticed the lead horse picking up speed. One by one the other horses followed. I knew what was coming next, tightened what few muscles in my legs would tighten, and gripped the saddle horn tightly with both hands. I felt Red start to change his gait to a trot.

> *"We need to learn from our painful experience. With pain comes change. With change comes growth."*

At first, the thrill of the speed delighted me. This was a new challenge and feeling of movement. Then I was aware of the jolting going on inside my body. I thought my internal organs were being permanently rearranged. I became conscious of my jaw movement and feared that I would bite my tongue. I clenched my teeth hard. The trotting continued and I closed my eyes, holding tightly onto the saddle horn, fearful of falling. My entire body bounced up and down on the saddle. My paralyzed legs and feet dangled along the sides of the horse.

After a few minutes the lead horse slowed to a walk. My horse followed. At last, I was safe. I forced a smile, reassuring Mark that I was fine. Little did I know that this series of gait changes from a slow walk to a fast trot would continue for the next hour.

Finally the hour-long ride was over. My thighs were aching and as I was helped off the horse, I welcomed the stability and comfort of my wheelchair.

When I got back to the lodge, I was shocked to see a dark spot on my left sock. I removed my shoe and sock and discovered that the stirrup had cut into my ankle and created a deep, bloody gash. I hadn't felt a thing.

Seeing the bloody gash, and not feeling any pain, was a weird experience. Since I have a spinal cord injury and my legs are paralyzed, I can't feel pain in certain areas of my body. I hadn't felt the pain to alert me that something was wrong and I needed to make a change.

I learned many lessons from this experience. First, there is no such thing as a slow trot! Second, do not let anyone else speak on my behalf. I should have spoken up when the tour guide asked Mark about the slow trot, and asked that the horse only walk. Third, I should have worn boots. Fourth, I became more aware that my body is more vulnerable to injury. Fifth and most important, I learned that pain can be a good thing.

Our bodies are amazing. When we feel pain, we need to recognize this as a warning that something is wrong. We need to make a change in order to make the pain go away. When pain cannot be felt, we are likely to be in more serious danger.

Each of us goes through painful experiences. Sometimes the pain is physical, while other times it is emotional. We need to learn from our painful experiences. With pain comes change. With change comes growth.

As we look back at our most painful experiences, we need to recognize what changes resulted and how we are better off now than we were before the pain. What is important is that we take the time to reflect. When we are in pain, we can learn from the experience and make the needed changes to avoid more pain in the future.

9

Life – It's Just Like Riding A Bike

Life's just like riding a bike. Once you've learned to ride a bike, you never forget. And once you've fallen off a bike, you've got to get back on. When life knocks you off your bike, you have to climb back on and "keep pedaling." I learned this the hard way when I had my accident.

Two months after I came home from the hospital, my home health aid accompanied me while I was giving a speech. She had never seen me perform in front of an audience, and when we returned home, she said, "Girl, you haven't lost it. You've still got it. It's just like riding a bike."

I had to laugh, as I was in a wheelchair because I fell off a bike. Later, I realized that she was telling me that my essence was intact. I was still me. When I speak to audiences, I can still impart knowledge and have a terrific relationship with them.

As I progress in my physical therapy, I see my legs getting stronger. Therapists taught me how to exercise and how to walk short distances with a walker, crutches and canes. As I saw my legs functioning again, I dreamed of activities that I could resume. One of my dreams was to bike again. In order to make this happen, I needed a special bike.

Adaptive recreational equipment is available for people with handicaps. Handcycles, footcycles, tandems and motor-assisted bikes make riding possible for those with limited use of their limbs, poor vision, head injury or difficulty in balancing. Some are bicycles, while others are tricycles.

After much research, my choice was a Trice recumbent tricycle that

I pedal with my legs. It was made in England.

Now, I can't wait to get up in the morning and go for a ride. I am independent again, cruising through my neighborhood. No longer do I have to depend on my husband, Mark, to push me in my wheelchair for a stroll after dinner.

My disability goes unnoticed as I pedal. The bike is a great disguise. No one would ever suspect that I am paralyzed, until they see me encountering steep terrain. The roads in my neighborhood are like the roads of life. Some are a smooth coast downhill, and others are a challenging uphill struggle.

The rolling ground beneath my wheels frequently changes in grade. I shift the trike into different gears to help me get up the inclines. Sometimes the strain is heavy as I struggle to make it up the hill. Sometimes I use my arms to help push on my legs.

As I monitor my speed, I am aware that I can go only about half as fast as I did before I was injured. My pace varies from one mile per hour on the steeper sections of our street to twelve miles per hour going down the other side.

So it is with life's challenges. Sometimes life seems like an uphill climb. We strain and toil and focus on reaching the top. From time to time we need to remind ourselves how badly we want to get there. Our drive and determination must be stronger than the challenges we face and sometimes we have to change into a higher gear to get the job done.

Occasionally, we "hit the wall" in athletic pursuits. We exert energy for as long as we think is possible, and then realize that there is no energy left. We stop. We lack momentum. We abandon the effort.

There will be times in your life where you come across this "wall." Obstacles, challenges and limitations will make success seem less likely. What we must remember is that momentum can be an energy force that gets you past the "wall." Once you are on a roll, keep moving. It is easier to make it up a difficult hill, or a difficult challenge, if we are already moving forward. Don't give up. Focus.

Downhill is the flip side of uphill; there can't be one without the other. Enjoy the downhill rides and appreciate the thrill of coasting. Life at any time can become difficult. It can just as suddenly become easy. It all depends on how well you're able to shift gears.

10

Patience is a Friend of Progress

Learning to do something differently can take what seems like forever. When I came home from the hospital five weeks after my spinal cord injury, I began learning the true meaning of patience. Patience is acceptance, a deep understanding that things take their own time.

You begin to have a different perspective on time when you are physically challenged and can no longer do things you used to do. Accepting my permanent disability and my newly limited abilities to care for myself took a lot of adjustment.

Completing even the simple tasks was a challenge. Getting out of bed, taking a shower, getting dressed, preparing a bowl of cereal, all took a large portion of my day. I needed a home health aide to assist me in all of these activities. No longer was I an independent, self sufficient person. Even with assistance, it took me two hours to shower and dress! The activity itself was so fatiguing, I was ready for a nap after the whole ordeal.

Sometimes changes occur in our lives that affect the way we do things in the future. Sudden injuries and illnesses make us appreciate all the things we took for granted. Sometimes we don't bounce back as quickly as we used to, and sometimes things change forever.

I have learned that I must allow more time to get things done and be patient with myself. Hurrying and struggling to complete tasks only brings frustration. Anger starts to swell inside, followed by depression. This cycle of negativity only leads to self-pity and self-neglect, a poor framework from which to operate.

Being patient with yourself allows you to be more conscious of how you do things. You are always in slow motion, analyzing and experimenting to see how to approach the task most efficiently. At first, you'll feel very incompetent, unable to perform. With more experience and time doing the task, you will begin to gain confidence. Eventually, you are unaware that you are performing the task. It has become effortless once again. The only difference is in the way you get it done.

In order to function adequately, I require adaptive aids such as a reacher, shower chair, canes, walker, crutches and wheelchair. But for me, taking on an attitude of "whatever it takes" propelled me to greater progress. Be open to changes and don't be resistant. Negative energy will slow you down even more.

> ***"I must not fear that time has passed, but must use each day to build a quality life for myself."***

As we grow to be more patient with ourselves, we need to have more patience with others. They must allot time to do things for us that we normally would do for ourselves. In many cases, there is a learning curve for our assistants. We must be patient and teach them what we want them to do for us.

Several years ago I saw a person wearing a T-shirt with this slogan: "Things of quality have no fear of time." What a relief those words brought me! I was now able to approach projects with a new sense of pride in my work.

Now, I adapt this phrase to my life in a new way. As I go through the recovery and rehabilitation process, two years after my injury, I realize that I *am* the project. Everything I do is focused on "getting my life back." I must not fear that time has passed, but must use each day to build a quality life for myself.

Success is sometimes best measured by spoonfuls. As we struggle with the changes in our lives, sometimes we are unaware of our accomplishments. Victories need to be celebrated, no matter how small the gain. It is critical that we look back from where we were days, weeks, months and years before so that we are more aware of our achievements.

As we recognize our progress, we become more patient with ourselves. Experience starts to show us that with dedication to our goals, gains can be made.

Count every achievement. Let those around you remind you from time to time to recognize your progress. Steady gains, in small increments, add up to big success over time.

11

Getting Comfortable in a New Pair of Shoes

Why is it that women typically own more shoes than men? How many pairs of black shoes does a woman really need? Women are typically teased for having so many pairs of shoes, and I am no exception. My shoe and boot collection has outgrown my closet space and has expanded to boxes in the basement.

Shoes serve many purposes; some are for fashion and some for comfort. Many have a specific athletic activity associated with the design.

When I was first paralyzed, I often thought of what my shoes and boots represented to me. I cried as I mourned my losses, knowing that I would never walk on the beach, tramp

> *"The possibility of regaining an active life with inactive feet seemed impossible."*

through the snow, dance, ride a horse, jog, roller blade, ski, play tennis or racquetball, take an aerobics class, or bike. My shoe and boot collection in my closets was a visual reminder of my overwhelming loss.

A few months after I had come home from the hospital, two girlfriends came over to help me rearrange my closets. It was hard for me to tell them to place my fashion, recreational and athletic shoes and boots in boxes to store in the basement.

It was especially painful seeing my biking shoes for the first time since my injury. I shuddered when I saw a dried leaf from the tree that crushed me, still clinging to the shoelaces.

In those early days, I never dreamed that I would put those shoes back on my paralyzed feet. The possibility of regaining an active life with inactive feet seemed impossible.

I didn't realize that I was limiting my own potential, and I was unaware of adaptive equipment and sports programs for the disabled. Over time, I investigated these options and learned to do many of my favorite sporting activities again.

In the three years since my injury, most of my shoes and boots have made their way back upstairs into my closet. I am grateful that my husband never donated them to a charity. Now I wear my shoes and boots when I dress up to go out, bike, ski, and ride a horse.

This week I went shopping for shoes. I rolled into a shoe store in my wheelchair and approached a male sales clerk. "I need to buy a pair of dressy black sandals to go with these dresses. Unlike most of your other customers, comfort doesn't matter. My feet are paralyzed."

The clerk's facial expression grew mournful and he looked down at the floor in silence. To break this awkward moment, I asked him to go to the back of the store and bring out shoes in my size. I then realized that I had more flexibility in shoe size as well as style, since comfort didn't matter. My selection criteria were simple – the shoes merely had to stay on my feet.

I placed shoes of several styles and heel heights on my feet. One pair had a strap that went across the back of my heel, allowing the shoe to stay in place. I told the clerk that I thought this pair would stay on my feet better when I went dancing at an upcoming black tie formal dance. He looked at me with a puzzled expression. I said, "I can dance now. It's different than before. I stand and put my arms around my partner's shoulders and keep my feet in one place as I sway gently to the music."

Since external foot comfort no longer matters to me, I must find ways to feel *internal* comfort. Now I take comfort in knowing that being different is acceptable. And when I fully accept the way things are now, I can also help raise the comfort level of others.

12

Asking for Help Is Not a Sign of Weakness

We all need help now and then. Financial, spiritual, physical and emotional help from others can get us through difficult times in our lives. Many of us are unable to recognize when help is needed, or are reluctant to ask for the help that others can provide.

As a very independent person, I wanted to do most things myself. I took care of my yard, cleaned my house, shopped for food and freely traveled for business and leisure activities. Then came the day when all that had to change.

The injury left me in a wheelchair, possibly for the rest of my life. To many, it is obvious by the wheelchair that I can use extra assistance. It is a visible symbol suggesting dependence. Early on, I became dependent on people for my very basic health needs. During two years of rehabilitation, I have seen tremendous progress and a return of my independence.

My first major milestone, about a year after I was injured, was driving my new minivan. The van is equipped with hand controls and a power ramp. The day I picked up the van, I drove for hours with no route or destination in mind. I just wanted to be free. Once again, I was free to move, free to decide where to go and how to get there.

Driving the van led me to more independence. I could drive to visit friends and family. I could drive just for the fun of it. I could get myself to business appointments and speaking engagements. I started to feel as if I were in the groove again!

In another milestone towards independence, I flew, by myself, from Columbus to Orlando, to deliver three days of training. My personal Independence Day had arrived. It had taken two years to develop the strength and skill set needed to get on an airplane, maneuver myself in the community, and care for myself in a hotel.

I was seldom really alone on this trip. People at the airport, airline, taxi service, hotel, restaurant and training facility all were eager to offer VIP service.

Doesn't it amaze you at times when people do things to help you? There are an overwhelming number of people in this world who are amazingly kind and thoughtful. Doing things to help other people makes us feel better. Oftentimes we feel honored that another person asked us for help. It is better to serve than to be served.

As I shared my story of the people who helped me on this trip, a high school friend at dinner replied, "Rosemarie, you bring out the best in people. You just give them a chance to be as good as they really are."

What's wrong with asking people for help? Asking for help is not a sign of weakness. Rather it shows that you know how to achieve your goal.

We are all dependent on others. Look around you at the services that are performed for you. Someone delivers your mail, newspaper and packages, hauls away your trash, provides your residence with utilities, maintains your car, and grows and processes your food. You depend on their services for your everyday living, but seldom think of yourself as being dependent.

All of us strive to find a balance between being independent and dependent. The point of balance will be different for each person. There is peace of mind in knowing that others will be there to help you when you are in need.

Our families and friends serve as the foundation of our support structure. Relying on each other enriches strong relationships, and gives family members a chance to bond as a team, to grow and to have new experiences.

Often we are afraid to ask for help. To many of us it is a sign that we are weak. We try to do it ourselves or else abandon our objective. By doing so, we are missing out on many opportunities, simply because we're afraid to ask others to lend a hand.

We must identify what we can do alone, and with limited or full assistance. Then, *ask*! It's that simple, ask! Don't jump to conclusions and assume that the person we want to ask will not be in a position to help. Wait until they reach this conclusion themselves. If they can't help, then ask if they know someone else who can. You owe it to yourself to ask until you hear a "Yes."

13

Having the Courage to Face Our Demons

Sometimes, a bad memory is tied to a specific location. Perhaps a crisis, dispute, death, injury or illness occurred in a particular place and you have not been able to return to it because of the bad memories it reawakens. Every time you think of, or drive near that site, you become emotional and purposely avoid going back.

That's how it was for me for the past two years. I purposely steered clear of the bicycle path in Granville, Ohio, where I was crushed by the falling tree.

This past March, a business trip brought me to Granville for the first time since I had been injured. I felt an avalanche of emotions as I drove my van past the entrance to the path. Then I pulled into the same spot I had parked in two years ago, turned off the ignition, and wept. The nightmare was returning.

> *"As we face our demons, we build the courage to stand up to what we fear."*

As I drove home, I thought about the sense of accomplishment I would feel if I could ride that trail again. I had been shopping for a bicycle I could pedal with my weakened legs and paralyzed feet and ankles. I had researched and tested several three wheeled recumbent trikes and found one that met my special needs. It was to be delivered in May.

On June 13, 2000, Mark and I set off for Granville. We were both uneasy about returning to our favorite trail. It also meant returning to the memories of the worst day of our lives.

Inevitably, deep emotions come to the surface when we return to a location where sadness prevailed. But this purging of emotional tensions can actually help us to heal those memories.

Mark and I rode to the exact spot where the tree had fallen on me. There we were, still alive and still in love. The dead tree lay where it had fallen. It was then that we were able to put many of the missing pieces together.

We could identify this site by the tree, the clearing in the woods where it had once stood, the spliced electric lines, the broken branches on the trees still standing, and logs cut from the tree that lay on the side of the trail. After riding on the trail and retracing the rescue operation, we better understood how hard the rescue team worked to get me out.

As we face our demons, we build the courage to stand up to what we fear. For me, the act of literally standing for the first time while clenching a walker was a courageous act.

In fact, I needed courage for so many of the tasks I have accomplished during the past two years. Regaining my life meant learning to do things all over again. It took courage to learn to drive a car with hand controls, to walk with crutches, to ski on a monoski, and to bike again.

Courage is the power to face your adversity. You are far more powerful than your outside circumstances, and once you recognize this, you will gain the courage you need to overcome anything.

After a setback, it is better for us to rejoice over our accomplishments than to dwell on self pity. What happened is in the past. It is more important that we focus on what is good in the present and our hopes for the future.

It seems as if we are sometimes dealt a hand of cards we prefer not to hold in the game of life. When that happens, we have many choices as to how to react. The best choice is to play out the hand, and wait for a better one next time.

14

Say Goodbye to Those Monday Blues

"Hangin' around, nothing to do but frown, rainy days and Mondays always get me down."

—*The Carpenters*

I always remember the lyrics from this song by The Carpenters. Sometimes we get the blues when circumstances overwhelm us. When we feel we have no control over the situation, we can get depressed for days at a time. Episodes of chronic depression can linger on, and sometimes we can't seem to get our spirit back.

Sometimes we can identify the problem and sometimes we can't. We feel lonely. We feel lousy. Eating patterns are disrupted. Sleep is elusive. We want to be alone and wallow in self pity.

Even while we feel sorrow and grief, we want it to go away. It is apparent that our normal work patterns have been altered and things pile up, making

> ## *"I decided to put a limit on 'crying' time."*

the situation worse. We long for happiness and want our lives to be productive. From my own experiences, I have learned that there are ways to reduce depression time.

- **Focus on a hopeful future, not on self pity.** As I became aware of the time I spent in self pity, I realized that self pity was leading to self neglect. I began to look terrible. My hair was a mess and I wasn't eating properly. I was isolating myself from people who would make me feel better. One day I discovered that by changing my thoughts, I could change the way I was feeling. I decided to put a limit on "crying" time. I found I could actually snap out of a slump at a predetermined time. I then turned my thoughts to a person, experience, or thing (like a rose) that made me feel better.

✔ Focus on a hopeful future, not on self pity.
✔ Get rest.
✔ Get exercise.
✔ Remove yourself from your environment.
✔ Make a conscious effort to have fun.
✔ Eat healthy.
✔ Do something for someone else.
✔ Monitor your medications.
✔ Get treatment.

• **Get rest.** Sometimes sleep patterns are interrupted and you'll need occasional naps. If so, lie down in a dark, quiet place where you will be undisturbed and sleep. It is amazing how much better you'll feel when you wake up.

• **Get exercise.** We know from experience and research that the body chemistry changes when we exercise. The changes result in a "high" feeling. Other advantages of exercise include better circulation and an enhanced intake of oxygen. Do whatever you can to exercise. Get your heart rate up. Take deep breaths. Even the simple act of walking in the mall or your neighborhood should make you feel better. Go to a health club and take advantage of the pool, weights, machines and aerobic classes. Play a sport that will give your muscles a workout. Sweat! It's good for you!

• **Remove yourself from your environment.** Get out of your house or apartment. Change your scenery. Go to a park. Take a drive. Go to the mall. See a friend. Occupy your mind with something else. Let your senses experience the world around you.

• **Make a conscious effort to have fun.** Now is the time to see a movie that will make you laugh, or go to a comedy club. Play video games, ride your bike, get on a swing, dance. Do things that you enjoy doing. Surround yourself with fun people.

• **Eat healthy.** We may unconsciously not be eating the right foods. We reach for the box of chocolates instead of a piece of fruit. We forage for "junk foods," high in fat, salt and sugars. Break the pattern and select foods from the food pyramid as recommended. Our bodies are fueled by the foods we eat, so give your body the best fuel for the energy you need. Stay away from alcohol.

• **Do something for someone else.** It's amazing how much my mood elevates when I'm helping someone else. Perhaps you can help someone in your family. Visit someone you know in the hospital or nursing home and offer to do something to comfort them.

See if your neighbor could use your help. Look for an opportunity to be useful.

• **Monitor your medications.** Drugs often have side-effects that depress your mood, make you lethargic, or make sleeping difficult. Read the labels of those prescriptions that you are taking and find out if they may be causing your depression. If so, talk to your doctor about alternatives.

• **Get treatment.** Medical intervention may be needed in long-term situations. Evidence shows, the most effective treatment for depression is a combination of medication with psychotherapy. See your doctor. The new antidepressant medications have fewer adverse side effects.

These tips may be useful to you now or in the future. If a crisis comes into your life without warning, it could lead to depression. It is important for us to have the knowledge to rebound.

As we interact with family and friends, we may notice that they too, have been down for an extended period of time. Talk to them and find out what you can do to help. When you find a way to lift their spirits and your own, you'll say goodbye to those Monday blues.

15

Making Changes, One Layer at a Time

Is there something about your life that makes you unhappy and that you feel you must change? Can you identify what you need to do to make change happen?

It's easy to resist making significant changes in our lives. We are comfortable with the way things are and don't want to expend the energy to change them. We seem to get in a groove and have tunnel vision regarding what we could do with our lives. We know that changes can be for the better, yet we often view change as scary, difficult, and time-consuming. We are fearful of the uncertain results.

Changes are needed as we go through life, and they can make a positive difference, both personally and professionally. But we must recognize that if we want our lives to change, then *we* have to change.

> *"...we must recognize that if we want our lives to change, then we have to change."*

We need to identify what changes are needed and have a vision of who we are, and who we want to become. For a start, you can make a list of the things that will make the most impact in your life if they were different. Focus on what will make you happy. Identify specific things you want to change, and then start an action plan.

Think of yourself as a woodcarver and your life as a block of wood to be crafted into a work of art. First, you'll need a vision of the finished piece. Then, you'll make rough sketches on the wood as a pattern and whittle away at the block, chipping off chucks of wood, and then removing thin layers. The first cuts make the biggest difference in appearance. As the carving process continues, changes are more subtle. Layer after layer, thin slices of wood are carved away until the piece is in its final form. Sandpaper is carefully used to buff and polish out the rough spots to add detail, luster, and texture to the piece. Now, you have transformed the wood from its original shape and sculpted it into a masterpiece.

In our lives, changes are also made one layer at a time. First, think of the changes you need in your life to make you happier. Then, start trimming the layers gradually. As with the artist who follows a pattern drawn on the block of wood, so should you change your life. Once you start changing from the surface layer of your being, the subtle changes that you initiate may be easier for you to accept. The transformation that you've made in your life may appear subtle at first, but over time you will begin to notice greater changes.

We are each a masterpiece, a composition made up of ideas, knowledge, creativity, intellect, personality, and experiences. Some of our talents lie dormant. When we polish our essence, and make it shine, we can model ourselves to reflect our fullest potential.

Recognize that like an artist, we can't make all the changes in one cut. We are a work in progress.

16

Dance with What You've Got

December 31, 1997. My husband, Mark, and I were dancing at a restaurant celebrating New Year's Eve. We were having the time of our lives, surrounded by family. I was in high heels and a stunning form fitting pant suit. Mark looked gorgeous as always.

I had no idea that this would be our last dance. Six months later, I was in a wheelchair. Today, Mark and I continue to celebrate New Year's Eves, but now we are dancing differently together.

After my injury, I fought to put my life back together. My love for dancing never left me, even though it appeared I would never dance or even walk beside Mark again. Both of us agreed that we missed dancing together. Mark and I had been taking dance lessons at the time of my injury and we had always looked forward to our times on the dance floor.

> *"By the time we finished our solo routine, Mark and I were breathless, and the room was hushed."*

I remember the first time I went on the dance floor after my injury with me in a wheelchair. I felt so self-conscious as people stared at me. Tears welled up in my eyes as I realized that I couldn't dance the way I used to. I knew, however, that I still wanted to be able to dance with Mark, and if it had to be in a wheelchair, so be it. We just needed to learn how to do it.

One day I was reading a magazine for people with disabilities, and saw an ad for a video on "wheelchair dancing." Excitedly, I showed it to

Mark who enthusiastically agreed that we should try it. Two weeks later, the video I ordered arrived, and after watching it, we were enchanted. Because we had credit at the local Fred Astaire Dance Studio, we called and talked to Louie, our former instructor. "Wheelchair dancing" was certainly new to him, but he agreed to teach us how, once he had taught himself, without using a wheelchair.

After five months of instruction, Mark and I were ready to try out our new dance routine. Louie had a special request: Would we perform our first dance showcase at the studio? "Of course," we agreed, grateful for Louie's continuing support. To our shock and amazement, fifty people showed up to watch us. Mark's confidence plummeted when he saw the others dancing, and was told by Louie to "Get out there with the rest of them!"

And we did.

By the time we were finished with our solo routine, Mark and I were breathless, and the room was hushed. Then, tears running down their cheeks, the audience rose to their feet and burst into applause.

Wheelchair dancing is gaining in popularity. There are videotapes available to show how the "wheeler" and "walker" work as partners. Dance studios are accepting clients in wheelchairs, and wheelchair users are participating in dance competitions. Now, when Mark and I go out on the dance floor, we spin with the best of them.

What have you got to dance with? You, too, can dance with whatever resources and abilities you have. And when you do, life will provide the music.

17

Discipline: A Key to Achieving Our Goals

Have you been thinking lately about what you want to accomplish this year? We all have periods in our lives when we decide to buckle down and work on our goals. We write them down and resolve to get them done. We talk about them with our friends, employers, and family. We have big plans that will propel our lives and our careers. We make "to do" lists. But, over time, nothing happens. We have great ideas and good intentions, but somehow we never quite achieve the progress that we aimed for.

We need to be able to prioritize our goals and recognize that there are two levels of priorities. One level of priority reflects goals that will have profound effects on our lives. The second level reflects goals that require our immediate attention.

For example, a goal that will have a profound effect on your life might be to get a new job. A goal that requires our immediate attention could be paying a long overdue bill. When we focus on the positive outcome of each goal, we can see how important it is to take care of both levels of goals.

I have come to realize that, regardless of the level of goal, a common missing link to progress is lack of discipline. We have not been diligent in sitting down at a pre-selected time to complete our tasks. We let other, less important tasks, take our time away from our higher priorities. Without realizing it, we have wasted time, and lost our energy and passion for our bigger plans.

I understand that I will never catch up. There are always things to do in my office and home. I could be productive and devote days to accomplishing less important tasks, and realize days later that I put off moving in the direction I needed to follow. I realize that this is a delaying tactic that many of us use without realizing it. Unfortunately this mode of procrastination can become habitual. It may take months for us to realize how we have sabotaged our efforts to reach our goals due to our lack of discipline.

In order to move ahead, we must change our patterns of operation. As we identify our goals, and their benefits, we must keep them in plain view. As an added incentive, we need to write down the consequences, missed opportunities, pain, and misfortunes that we will experience if we do not pursue our stated goals.

As you begin a project, select a date and time when you expect to have the project completed. Make a commitment to yourself, and if appropriate, make this commitment to others who are affected by the outcome of this project. You will be amazed at how your subconscious mind processes information that will be useful to you as you tackle the task at hand. Self-imposed deadlines do work!

Get yourself mentally and physically ready for the task ahead. Realize that you'll be expending energy, and that your mind and body need to be at their peak. It is wise to get adequate rest and nutrition prior to starting any sizable project.

In order to discipline yourself, select the time that you will start and stop the task. Consider this an unbreakable appointment, and allow no interruptions to side track you. As you get involved with the project, and the time that you have set aside is ending, decide if it is best to extend the time, or stop working on the project.

> *"We need to be able to prioritize our goals and recognize that there are two levels of priorities."*

Start working on the biggest, hardest, most imposing task first. Get your highest level of energy behind you and work towards this accomplishment. Power yourself and stay with it until you have completed this task. As you accomplish these seemingly more difficult tasks, the other tasks will appear less daunting

Often, the momentum it took to get started is a great source of energy that fuels your efforts to make continued progress. You may find that the task can be completed in a shorter time than you originally planned. Setting time limits for your tasks allows you to be a better judge of whether the time invested is worth the benefits you expect to receive.

The cornerstones of personal achievement are goal setting, focus, commitment, and discipline. Acknowledging these as your base of support, will allow you to recognize your limitations and make the adjustments necessary to enhance your life.

18

When We Live in the Future,
We Miss Out on Today

Preoccupation with the future robs us of today. When we have something to look forward to we take great joy in anticipating the future. As we wake up in the morning and look ahead, mentally reviewing our calendars, we are eager to face the day, the week, and the month. As the time for the enjoyable event gets closer, we become more excited.

Sometimes this anticipation of future events and activities comes at the expense of living in the moment. We get preoccupied with thoughts of our future, yet there is no guarantee there will *be* a future. We plan for future events and focus on how we can make them successful, while never fully appreciating what is currently going on around us. Sometimes thoughts of tomorrow overtake the pleasures of today.

Have you ever caught yourself face to face with another person while your thoughts were somewhere else? We sometimes cheat ourselves of important conversations in the moment as our minds focus on other things that we could be doing. The person we are talking to has no idea of our thoughts, yet we are no longer appreciating the conversation. We aren't paying attention and we aren't listening.

The words and actions of others should command our full attention. We need to be consciously aware of the present, and enjoy our present activities.

We need not rush the future, for it will be here soon enough. As I think back over the last three years since my paralyzing injury, there were many times when I had questions about my future.

Would I ever walk again? Dance again? Have the full use of my body again? Something inside me said, "Yes! Don't give up!" Now every day, I anticipate a better future, with medical advances that will restore what I have lost.

I have met others with disabilities who do not have a positive outlook on life. They talk as if their conditions and losses are forever. We must realize that medical specialists anticipate finding solutions to medical problems. These scientists, doctors, and researchers are hopeful that their study, investigation, and research of medical problems will lead to eliminating diseases, healing injuries, and finding cures in the near future. The medications, treatments, therapy, adaptive devices and equipment that we use today can often improve our conditions.

> ## "We need not rush the future, for it will be here soon enough."

When people ask me if I can walk, I explain that I can walk short distances if I use adaptive devices like a walker, crutches, or canes. I am also hopeful that a cure will be found for spinal cord injury that will enable my body to fully function once more. Having a hopeful future helps me to be optimistic, and allows me to live my life with the conviction that my body will one day be restored.

Think about what limitations you are experiencing and how you are currently thinking about your future. Do you anticipate better days ahead? Do you believe your conditions are permanent? Are you following the advances in medical science and anticipating progress that can be directly applied to you? Or are you preoccupied with negative thoughts of your future and unable to enjoy the hours today?

Life presents us with choices. It is far better to appreciate the positive aspects of our lives and our relationships with others, than to wallow in self-pity. We must remember that we have the freedom to think, to dream, and to hope for anything we want. Why not make it positive, hopeful, and healing?

19

Seeing the 'Possible' Requires True Vision

Sometimes seeing, isn't believing. Have you ever casually glanced at something, only to stare in amazement, trying to figure out what you were seeing? You couldn't believe your eyes. I had one of these moments recently.

Last week, I was on vacation in San Francisco. My husband, Mark, pushed me in my wheelchair along the water's edge at Fisherman's Wharf. As we strolled by the rocky beach, we saw a man crouched by a column of three rocks. These rocks were of different sizes, carefully balanced, one on top of the other. The largest rock, about two feet tall, was on the bottom. The smallest rock, about four inches tall, was in the middle, and another large, two foot tall rock was on the top.

At first I thought this was a piece of artwork that had cement between each rock to hold it in position. The more I looked at the column, and at the man who was in the act of creating a second column of rocks, the more I realized that each rock was carefully balanced and was not held in place by cement. The column of rocks seemed to defy the laws of gravity. I thought to myself, "Certainly this column of rocks will tumble. That's impossible!" As I watched in amazement, the two columns remained steadfastly in place.

This balancing act appeared impossible to Mark and me. The man who positioned the rocks had another vision of possibility in his mind's eye. He knew that what others perceived as "impossible" was indeed, possible.

That's how it is in life. In our minds, we often view activities and projects as impossibilities and rule out success without even trying. At other times, if at first we don't succeed, we might give up.

We need to think back to the times when the impossible dream *did* come true in our lives. We have all had lucky breaks, unlikely successes, and unexpectedly happy endings. What made them different? Why did things turn out right? What made the impossible appear to be possible?

I am amazed at the progress that I have made since my spinal cord injury two and a half years ago. When I left the hospital, I could barely lift my legs while seated in the wheelchair. Walking seemed totally impossible to me. Today, I walk into my health club three days a week, using leg braces and a rolling walker. Last fall, I walked a mile. Last summer, I rode my three-wheeled bicycle 18 miles. I can only wonder what milestones lay ahead. I know I must not fall prey to resting on my accomplishments. After all, the "impossible" is just likely to be possible!

My dedication to rehabilitation made progress possible. Hard work and persistence paid off. Going to physical therapy three days a week for two years, resulted in my present achievements.

What I have learned is that we sometimes foresee our future less optimistically than we should. We procrastinate, have low self-esteem, are in a state of self-pity, and think that we just can't make things happen. Think again!

Let this image of possibility be the focus of your life. Tough times don't last forever. Situations change, and improve for the better. Help is available if only we ask for it. We need to take charge of our lives and circumstances, and be more proactive in order for our situations to improve.

The next time I am faced with a challenge, I will remember the image of the column of rocks. We need not be so quick to judge the challenge as an impossibility, but rather realize that the impossible may someday become reality.

20

Living Life with Conviction

Life is like a roller coaster. There are hills to climb and hills to coast. Your image of your life is critically important to your success. Although we are in control of many of the circumstances around us, there are other circumstances beyond our control.

We all go through setbacks, changes, disappointments, crisis and tragedies. We need to be able to triumph over tragedy. As I have struggled to take back my life after a major, life-changing injury, I have learned that if I want things to change, *I* have to make the changes.

Adjusting to life after a crisis seems insurmountable. To succeed, you'll require hard work, dedication, commitment, a determined spirit and a firm belief that you can accomplish your goals. There are no shortcuts to meaningful accomplishments.

You can transform your life from a state of total frustration and hopelessness to an impassioned state of determination. It's true by the way, that in the words of Robert Schuller, "Tough times never last, but tough people do."

We all have within us an inexhaustible reserve of potential that we have never even come close to realizing. Within us is a reserve of energy, courage, intelligence, ability and creativity that is waiting to be tapped.

> *"Living with conviction means living with passion, knowing that every day is precious."*

Living with conviction requires a positive vision of your future;

seeing hope rather than hopelessness. Examine the purpose of your life and focus on your main goal. For me, my main goal is getting my life back. I want to regain function and resume my career and all the activities that I enjoyed so much before I was injured. I need to remind myself each day to work at my goals. Progress moves me closer to my goals each day.

As I monitor my goals and accomplishments, I keep track of my progress. I set new personal best records. As I repeat the activity I try to smash my previous record, overcome limitations and break through my own barriers.

Living with conviction means living with passion, knowing that every day is precious. We get one shot, and one shot only, at each day we're given. Let's be sure it's the very best effort we can make.

Rosemarie's Lessons to Live By

1. *Do something new every day.*

2. *Focus on a hopeful future, not on self pity.*

3. *Believe that the impossible just might be possible.*

4. *Allow more time to get things done and be patient with yourself.*

5. *To lower your stress, lower your expectations of other people.*

Rosemarie Rossetti, Ph.D.
www.RosemarieSpeaks.com
Rosemarie@RosemarieSpeaks.com

About Rosemarie Rossetti, Ph.D.

An experienced author, syndicated columnist, professional motivational speaker, trainer and consultant, Rosemarie tells her unprecedented story from the time of her spinal cord injury through her recovery. On June 13, 1998, she was paralyzed when an 80-foot tree, weighing 3-1/2 tons, fell on her while she was riding her bicycle.

Since her injury, Rosemarie has shared the lessons she learned and her commitment to live her life with strength and conviction. In January 2002, she carried the Winter Olympic torch in Columbus, Ohio. One of more than 210,000 people nominated, Rosemarie was selected for her ability to inspire others. In February, 2002, she was a finalist in the Ms. Wheelchair Ohio competition.

Rosemarie now writes a monthly syndicated column with a readership of 31,000. "Take Back Your Life!" is a special collection of her readers' favorite columns.

In the book, "Mission Possible!" she was joined by other mission-minded authors, including Stephen Covey, Deepak Chopra, Les Brown and Pat Summitt. All of these authors have overcome personal challenges and have taken their messages to others facing growth experiences.

As a nationally known motivational speaker, her message is focused on coping with change and how to successfully deal with adversity.

To receive free by e-mail, the most recent inspirational articles each month, subscribe at: www.RosemarieSpeaks.com.

Quick Order Form

Thank you for your order. A portion of the proceeds will be donated to a Spinal Cord Injury Research Fund at The Ohio State University.

To learn about Rosemarie Rossetti's speaking business, or to order books on-line, visit her web site.

Web orders: http://www.RosemarieSpeaks.com

Fax orders: 614-471-5575

Postal orders: Rossetti Enterprises Inc.
1008 Eastchester Drive
Columbus, OH 43230-6230

Name: _____

Address: _____

City: _____ State: _____ Zip: _____

Phone: _____

E-mail address: _____
(Provide your e-mail address to receive Rosemarie's free monthly inspirational article.)

Payment Information:

☐ Check (payable to *Rossetti Enterprises Inc.*)

☐ Purchase Order #_____

☐ Visa   ☐ MasterCard   ☐ AMEX   ☐ Discover

Card Number: _____ Exp Date: _____

Name on Card: _____

Number of books:	
Total purchase price:	
6.75 % sales tax: (Ohio residents only)	
Total enclosed:	

Number of Books	Price (includes shipping)
1	$12.50
5	$57.50
10	$110.00
15	$157.50
20	$200.00
Larger volume discounts available	